RECORD BUSTERS
DINOSAURS
CLIVE GIFFORD

Printed in 2015

ISBN: 978 0 7502 8861 3
Library ebook ISBN: 978 0 7502 8505 6

Wayland
An imprint of
Hachette Children's Group
Part of Hodder & Stoughton
Carmelite House
50 Victoria Embankment
London EC4Y 0DZ

Editor: Nicola Edwards
Designer: Basement 68

10 9 8 7 6 5 4 3 2

First published in 2014 by Wayland

Printed in China

An Hachette UK Company

www.hachette.co.uk

www.hachettechildrens.co.uk

Picture credits:

The author and publisher would like to thank the following for allowing their images to be reproduced in this publication: Cover: Shutterstock DM7; p3 Shutterstock © Andreas Meyer; p4 Shutterstock © leonello calvetti; p5 (t) Shutterstock © Leonello Calvetti, (b) UIG via Getty Images; p6 Shutterstock © Linda Bucklin; p7 Shutterstock © Catmando; p8 Richard Nowitz (National Geographic); p9 Shutterstock © Catmando; pp10-11 Shutterstock © DM7; p12 (l) Shutterstock © Andreas Meyer, (r) Wikimedia Commons; p13 Daniel Eskridge/Stocktrek Images; p14 Shutterstock © Troyka; p15 (t) Shutterstock © Michael Rosskothen, (b) Antonio Scorza/AFP/Getty Images; p16 Craig Brown/ Stocktrek Images; p17 (t) Kabacchi, (b) Nobu Tamura; p18 (l) Woudloper, (r) Natural History Musuem; p19 Kabacchi; p20 Jacques Demarthon/AFP/Getty Images; p21 Shutterstock © Catmando; p22 (l) Shutterstock © Michael Rosskothen, (r) Wikimedia Commons; p23 UIG via Getty Images; p24 Shutterstock © Andreas Meyer; p25 (t) Shutterstock © Michael Rosskothen, (b) Captmondo; p26 DEA PICTURE LIBRARY; p27 Shutterstock © Leonello Calvetti; p28 Shutterstock © Leonello Calvetti; p29 (t) Quadell, (b) Captmondo; p30 Shutterstock © Catmando

Abbreviations used:

m = metres
km = kilometres
cm = centimetres
g = grammes
kg = kilogrammes
km/h = kilometres per hour

Tricky words are listed in 'But What Does That Mean?' on page 31.

WHAT'S INSIDE?

ANKYLOSAURUS

Ankylosaurus was built like a tank with heavy bony plates all over its body. It had triangular horns on its head and large ridges made of bone on its back to help protect it against attacks.

MOST ARMOURED DINOSAUR!

Can you believe it?

The dinosaur's only weak spot was its soft underbelly, so attackers would try to flip it over onto its back. Not easy, when an adult Ankylosaurus weighed over four tonnes!

At around 6-6.5m long, an Ankylosaurus was built like a small, armoured van.

Ankylosaurus had a giant tail shaped like a sledgehammer made of tough, heavy bone. Swung by powerful muscles, this club would have smashed bones when it struck.

WOW!

ONE TYPE OF ANKYLOSAUR, CALLED EUOPLOCEPHALUS, EVEN HAD BONY, ARMOURED EYELIDS!

An adult Ankylosaurus had a wide, low-slung body, with tough, leathery skin.

SAUROPOSEIDON

Sauropods were the biggest of all dinosaurs, each with four thick legs and an enormous body. With its giant neck, Sauroposeidon could stand 20m high. That's as high as a six-floor building!

Can you believe it?

Sauroposeidon weighed at least 40 tonnes and needed a 200kg heart to pump blood around its body. Its 11m-long neck allowed it to eat parts of trees that other dinosaurs couldn't reach.

Mighty Sauroposeidon lived around 110 million years ago in what is now North America.

CONTENDERS

Diplodocus was not as tall with a 5-6m-high neck, but may have been longer – up to 35m. Brachiosaurus had a 7m-long neck and may have reared up on its front legs to reach high tree branches.

WOW!

DIPLODOCUS' TAIL WAS ABOUT 14M LONG AND, WHEN FLICKED, MAY HAVE MADE A SHATTERING SOUND, LIKE THE CRACKING OF A HUGE WHIP.

A herd of Diplodocus dinosaurs graze as they pass through a forest.

STRUTHIOMIMUS

The speediest dinosaur so far found would have looked like a gigantic ostrich. Struthiomimus was about 4.3m long and weighed as much as two or three people. It could run at speeds of 60 to 80km/h.

FASTEST RUNNER!

Can you believe it?

As much as half of Struthiomimus' weight may have been muscle. It needed huge muscles to run at such high speeds. Dinosaur experts believe it may have used its speed to escape from dinosaur predators.

The Struthiomimus may have used its long tail to help it balance as it ran fast.

On the other hand...

Giant four-legged dinosaurs like Brachiosaurus and Sauroposeidon moved much more slowly – plodding along and moving their heavy bodies at less than 4km/h.

A Brachiosaurus was over 20m long and a slow mover.

WOW!

WHEN STRUTHIOMIMUS WAS RUNNING FAST, IT WOULD HAVE TAKEN 8-9M-LONG STRIDES.

TYRANNOSAURUS REX

The most famous of all dinosaurs, Tyrannosaurus Rex is a record buster for its bite. Scientists think its huge neck and jaws were moved by enormous muscles. These gave it enormous bite pressure, which meant it was able to crush flesh and bone. The T-Rex could have crushed a small car with its jaws!

STRONGEST BITE!

The T-Rex's massive jaw contained as many as 60 conical-shaped teeth, each up to 40cm long.

Its fearsome teeth meant that a T-Rex could grip and rip the flesh of its prey.

CONTENDERS

Gigantosaurus was another powerful predator, bigger than T-Rex but with not quite such powerful jaws.

Scientists estimate that a T-Rex had more power in its bite than 15 lions!

UTAHRAPTOR

Raptors were a type of two-legged dinosaur. Most were fierce but small. Utahraptor, though, was much larger. It was up to 7m long and stood 1.8m tall at its hips.

BIGGEST RAPTOR!

Can you believe it?

Utahraptor lived around 125 million years ago. It must have terrified other dinosaurs with its large jaws full of teeth and its powerful legs, which allowed it to run fast (25-35km/h) in short bursts.

UP CLOSE

Utahraptor had a 20-24cm-long claw on the second toes of its feet. This may have been used for slashing and hooking into the hide of an animal it attacked.

All four of Utahraptor's limbs ended in sharp claws.

WOW!

THE MOST FAMOUS RAPTORS, VELOCIRAPTORS, ARE SOMETIMES SHOWN IN MOVIES TOWERING OVER HUMANS. IN FACT THEY WOULD ONLY REACH YOUR WAIST AND WERE THE SIZE OF A TURKEY.

Small but fierce, Velociraptors lived in central Asia.

QUETZALCOATLUS

Flying reptiles were called Pterosaurs. The biggest of all was Quetzalcoatlus. It measured up to 11 or 12m from wingtip to wingtip. Its wings were layers of skin and had no feathers.

LARGEST WINGSPAN!

A giant Quetzalcoatlus. Its skull alone would have been around 80cm long.

Can you believe it?

Quetzalcoatlus' wingspan was the same as many World War II fighter planes. It is almost four times wider than the biggest bird alive today, the albatross.

On the other hand...

Nemicolopterus was a tiny Pterosaur, first discovered in China. It had a wingspan of around 25cm, not much bigger than a house sparrow.

Nemicolopterus had no teeth but claws which probably allowed it to grip tree branches.

SPINOSAURUS

Move over T-Rex! There's a bigger meat-eating two-legged dinosaur on the block and it's called Spinosaurus. It lived around 97 to 112 million years ago and grew to between 13m and 18m long.

Can you believe it?

Spinosaurus was longer than a bus. It had a series of giant spines on its back covered in skin to form a sail shape.

Spinosaurus had three claws on its hand, including a thumb claw which was used for poking or stabbing.

WOW!

SPINOSAURUS' JAWS WERE UP TO 1.7M LONG, ABOUT THE SAME SIZE AS A BATHTUB. THE DINOSAUR MAY HAVE USED THEM IN SHALLOW WATER TO CATCH HUGE 3M-LONG FISH.

A full-size Spinosaurus model skeleton shows the 1.65m-tall spines that stuck up from its backbone.

On the other hand...

Discovered in Canada, Hesperonychus Elizabethae is one of the smallest known dinosaurs that hunted and ate meat. It was only about the size of a small chicken.

Hesperonychus weighed no more than 2kg and was covered in feathers.

THERIZINOSAURUS

Therizinosaurus is an odd-shaped dinosaur discovered in Mongolia in 1948. It had a beak like a bird, a big pot belly and giant claws. Each claw measured between 70cm and 100cm long!

BIGGEST CLAWS!

Can you believe it?

Dinosaur experts believe that Therizinosaurus used its claws to grip and slash branches as well as stripping bark from trees for food. It may have used its claws for self-defence as well.

Therizinosaurus' claws were at the end of their 2.5-3.5m-long arms.

Monster claws and small sharp teeth made Megaraptor a scary predator.

CONTENDERS

Megaraptor had a giant claw that was 30cm long on each of its hands. The dinosaur lived around 85 million to 90 million years ago.

19

CERATOPSIANS

Ceratopsians were a group of four-legged dinosaurs including Triceratops. They ate plants using large, parrot-like beaks and had enormous heads complete with a bony frill. They also had massive horns for defence.

BIGGEST HORNS!

Can you believe it?

The head of a Triceratops was over 2m long, and featured three horns. There was a short one on its nose and two hefty horns above its eyes. These grew up to 1m long.

A Triceratops skull was sturdy and heavy. It weighed around 270kg!

Coahuilaceratops was around 7m long and stood 2m tall.

CONTENDERS

Torosaurus had horns around the same size as Triceratops. A new dinosaur called Coahuilaceratops was recently discovered in Mexico. It may have had even longer horns, about 1.25m long.

ARGENTINOSAURUS

Argentinosaurus lived in South America around 95 million years ago. Dinosaur experts estimate that it was 25m-30m long and weighed as much as 80 tonnes – more than 12 elephants or 1,000 people!

HEAVIEST DINOSAUR!

Argentinosaurus may have reached around 8m in height.

Can you believe it?

Single bones in a spine or backbone are called vertebrae. In humans, they measure a few centimetres across. A single vertebra from Argentinosaurus has been discovered which is 159cm wide.

WOW!

ARGENTINOSAURUS LAID EGGS A LITTLE SMALLER THAN A RUGBY BALL. THE YOUNG MUST HAVE GROWN REALLY FAST. A YOUNG ADULT WOULD HAVE EATEN MORE THAN 250KG OF FOOD A DAY!

On the other hand...

Compsognathus only weighed about 2kg-3kg when fully grown but there are even lighter dinosaurs. These include Parvicursor (less than 300g) and Epidexipteryx, which weighed about 165g.

Compsognathus ran low to the ground and was only about 1m long from tail to snout.

ELASMOSAURUS

Plesiosaurs were a type of underwater reptile that lived at the same time as dinosaurs. Elasmosaurus was one of the very longest. It was around 14m long and weighed 2,200kg. Its neck was about 8m long – the length of a bus!

LONGEST-NECKED PLESIOSAUR!

Can you believe it?

The neck contained 71 bones. The creature could only move slowly in water but it could move its long neck and head around quickly to snatch fish and other sea creatures for food.

Elasmosaurus moved through the water powered by its four large paddles.

On the other hand...

Liopleurodon had next to no neck, but it did have a long snout full of razor-sharp teeth, some more than 25cm long, to snap up other sea creatures.

More than 50 razor-sharp teeth lined the powerful jaws of a Liopleurodon.

WOW!

OPHTHALMOSAURUS HUNTED IN THE DARK, USING ITS ENORMOUS EYES, WHICH WERE ABOUT 23CM WIDE, TO FIND PREY.

TROODON

Most dinosaurs had very small brains for their giant size. Troodon was a small dinosaur about 2.5m long. But it had one of the biggest brains – about the size of a small orange.

Can you believe it?

Troodon had large eyes, around 4-5cm in size. It used these together with its brain to spot and track smaller creatures, which it hunted and ate.

Troodon fossils have been found inside the Arctic Circle. This may make it the most northerly dinosaur as well as the brainiest!

WOW!

DINOSAUR EXPERTS BELIEVE THAT TROODON COULD RUN AT SPEEDS OF UP TO 48KM/H.

On the other hand...

Scientists think that Stegosaurus may have been a bit of a dinosaur dunce! This heavy, four-legged dinosaur was about the size of a truck but it had a tiny brain, no bigger than a walnut.

A Stegosaurus may have weighed over 4 tonnes but its brain may only have weighed 80-100g.

EDMONTOSAURUS

Edmontosaurus was the toothiest of all dinosaurs. Found in North America, it had around 1,000 teeth in its long mouth. An adult human usually has 32!

MOST TEETH!

Can you believe it?

Edmontosaurus' teeth were shaped like diamonds. It used them to grind up plants, twigs and seeds as food.

Edmontosaurus needed to eat a lot every day as it grew up to 13m long.

WOW!

EDMONTOSAURUS HAD A SPECIAL HINGE JOINT IN ITS SKULL. THIS ALLOWED IT TO MOVE ITS JAWS FROM SIDE TO SIDE TO GRIND DOWN TOUGH FOOD.

Replacement teeth grew in an Edmontosaurus mouth to take over from those that had worn down.

CONTENDERS

Nigersaurus had a strange shaped head with a wide mouth like a postbox slot. It contained 500 or more teeth that acted like a lawnmower, cutting and eating grass and small plants on the ground.

The long row of teeth in a Nigersaurus skull would have sheared off plants at ground level.

29

TEST YOURSELF!

Can you remember facts about the record-busting dinosaurs in this book? Test yourself here by answering these questions!

1. Which dinosaur had large horns on its head: Elasmosaurus, Stegosaurus or Triceratops?

2. How long was Megaraptor's giant claw?

3. Which dinosaur had the biggest eyes, Troodon, Hesperonychus Elizabethae or Ophthalmosaurus?

4. Which dinosaur lived the longest time ago: Argentinosaurus, Utahraptor or Spinosaurus?

5. Which dinosaur had giant claws up to one metre long?

6. Which was longer: Quetzalcoatus' wingspan or Elasmosaurus' neck?

7. About how much did an Argentinosaurus weigh?

8. Which dinosaur looked like a large ostrich and could run very fast?

9. Which dinosaur had a large, wide mouth filled with 500 teeth: Elasmosaurus, Nigersaurus or Ankylosaurus?

10. Which dinosaur had the strongest bite?

Answers

1. Triceratops
2. 3ocm
3. Ophthalmosaurus
4. Utahraptor
5. Therizinosaurus
6. Quetzalcoatus' wingspan
7. 80 tonnes
8. Struthiomimus
9. Nigersaurus
10. Tyrannosaurus Rex

BUT WHAT DOES THAT MEAN?

armoured Covered in some sort of hard bone or tough material that protects the dinosaur's body.

bite pressure The amount of force with which a set of jaws and teeth can press together.

conical Shaped like a cone with a circular base rising up and sloping inwards to form a point.

fighter plane A type of attacking aircraft used by air forces which usually has seats inside for just one or two crew members.

fossils The remains of creatures or plants preserved in rock.

frill A wide border around the head of some dinosaurs, made of bone or tough fibres.

plates Flat or nearly flat bony panels that covered the body of some dinosaurs.

pot belly A large, rounded stomach.

predator A creature that hunts and eats other creatures.

prey The creatures that a predator hunts and attacks for food.

reptiles Cold-blooded creatures covered in bony plates or scales including lizards, crocodiles and dinosaurs.

scythe A large curved blade used to cut down grass or crops like wheat.

self defence When a creature fights to defend itself from another creature which has attacked it.

skull A case made of bone that forms a creature's head and protects the brain inside it.

sledgehammer A heavy stone or metal hammer.

snout The part of a creature's face which sticks out at the front and contains the nose, mouth and jaw.

vertebrae Bones that form the spine or backbone.

wingspan The distance across a creature's wings when they are stretched out.

CHECK IT OUT & INDEX

Check out these amazing places to go and websites to visit!

National History Museum, London, England
Meet a terrifying T-Rex and lots more dinosaurs!

National Dinosaur Museum, Canberra, Australia
See the real skeletons of more than 20 dinosaurs.

Wyoming Dinosaur Centre, Thermopolis, USA
Be wowed by Stegosaurus, Triceratops and Velociraptors at this museum.

The Dinosaur Museum, Dorchester, England
Here you can discover lots of fossils and full-size models of many dinosaurs, including Triceratops.

http://www.kidsdinos.com/
Learn more about dinosaurs at this great site.

http://www.nhm.ac.uk/kids-only/dinosaurs/index.html
This section of the Natural History Museum's website has lots of features on dinosaurs.

http://www.bbc.co.uk/nature/collections/pookf6gd
Watch amazing videos from the BBC showing reconstructions of dinosaurs in action.

Index